Changing Britain

vol 2: 1970 to modern times

A late 1970s Atari 2600 console.

A toy ET inspired by the 'ET' movie 1982.

Curriculum Visions

There's much more on-line including videos

You will find multimedia resources covering a wide range of topics at:

www.CurriculumVisions.com

CurriculumVisions is a subscription web site.

A CVP Book
Copyright © Atlantic Europe Publishing 2008–2010

First edition 2008. Revised edition 2010.

The right of Brian Knapp to be identified as the author of this work has been asserted by him in accordance with the Copyright, Designs and Patents Act 1988.

Author
Brian Knapp, BSc, PhD

Senior Designer
Adele Humphries, BA, PGCE

Editor
Gillian Gatehouse

Illustrations
Mark Stacey

Designed and produced by
Atlantic Europe Publishing

Printed in China by
WKT Company Ltd

Changing Britain vol 2: 1970 to modern times
Revised Edition – Curriculum Visions
A CIP record for this book is available from the British Library

ISBN 978 1 86214 639 6

Picture credits
All photographs are from the Earthscape Picture Library except the following: (c=centre t=top b=bottom l=left r=right)
Alamy page 4–5; NASA page 18b; ShutterStock pages 4bl, 5bl, 12, 15r, 23br, 24l, 27bl, 42, 47; TopFoto pages 6br, 10, 13, 18tr, 19, 24–25 (main), 27t, 28–29 (main), 31tr, 34; TopFoto/HIP page 7r; TopFoto/Image Works page 43tr; TopFoto/Keystone page 43br; www.raleighchopper.info page 15tl.

The publishers have made their best endeavours to contact all copyright holders for material published in this book.

This product is manufactured from sustainable managed forests. For every tree cut down at least one more is planted.

A music cassette.

Contents

Words in **BOLD CAPITALS** are further explained in the glossary on page 48.

Note: in this book the term 'Britain' is used as a shorthand, meaning "The United Kingdom of Great Britain and Northern Ireland".

1980s 'New Romantics' singles.

Band Aid's 1984 single.

A late 1990s Furby.

A 1989 Game Boy and cartridge (left) and an early 21st century Nintendo DS Lite cartridge (right).

A Nintendo Wii remote, 2007.

The 1970s

It was a time when many workers went on strike, when people at home and work had to use candles because there was no electricity, and when prices rose very quickly. The term 'Winter of Discontent' summed it all up.

In the 1960s, Britain had been a prosperous country. The Prime Minister, Harold Macmillan, said, "You have never had it so good". It was the time of the 'Swinging Sixties', the miniskirt and hippies (see *'Changing Britain vol 1: 1948–69'*).

In the 1970s it all started to go horribly wrong. People wanted higher wages, but they didn't want to work harder or change the ways they worked. The quality of what they made went down.

1 During the 'Winter of Discontent' ...led up on the streets

Our cars, for example, were unreliable and the bodywork rusted. Buildings – especially skyscraper homes – were put up cheaply and they were unpleasant to live in. At the same time, people in countries overseas started making things cheaper and better than us. What we needed was a 'wake up call', but it did not happen in the 1970s.

1970s timeline

Beatles break up. Computer floppy disks introduced.

Pocket calculators introduced. Bloody Sunday massacre in Northern Ireland. David Bowie is Ziggy Stardust.

The 3-day week and miners' strike. Provisional IRA bombing campaign in England. Israel-Arab war cuts fuel supplies worldwide and Britain introduces rationing cards for petrol.

1970 | **1971** | **1972** | **1973** | **1974**

Beginnings of English punk. Britain changes to decimal currency, metric weight and length, and out go pounds, shillings and pence, pounds and ounces. First VCRs are sold.

Britain becomes a member of the Common Market (now EU). Pink Floyd makes the album, 'Dark side of the Moon'. Widespread strikes.

power stations, and electricity had to be rationed. Most homes and offices had to use candles for lighting. Factories were told to operate only three-day weeks to save electricity, but even this did not help. Eventually, the government lost the battle, and although people went back to work, their wages went up for no extra work.

The demand for more and more money for no extra work carried on through the 1970s. In 1978–79 many people went on strike again. This time there was no-one to collect rubbish (picture ①), to fight fires, or even to bury the dead. This is what became known as the 'Winter of Discontent'.

At the end of 1979, the government gave up and elections were held. This is when Margaret Thatcher was elected the first woman prime minister (see also '1980s' section, page 19). She became one of Britain's most famous prime ministers, promising the people who were fed up with strikes that she would change everything. And she did.

Hard times for Labour

During the 1970s, the government had to battle against **TRADE UNIONS** who wanted more money for no extra work. In 1973 the government refused to pay more and many people, including coal miners, went on **STRIKE**. Soon there was not enough coal for

---

Microsoft founded (which now makes the Windows operating system found on most PCs).

Queen Elizabeth's Silver Jubilee.
Elvis Presley found dead.
'Star Wars' film is released in the UK.

Margaret Thatcher first British woman prime minister.
Sony introduces the Walkman.

1975   **1976**   **1977**   **1978**   **1979**

Supersonic airliner Concorde 'takes off'.
Iceland and Britain fight the cod war over fish supplies in the Atlantic Ocean.

First test-tube baby born'
First 'Hitchhiker's guide to the Galaxy' programme goes out on radio.
'Winter of Discontent' with many people on strike.

Music in the 1970s

During the 1970s, the Beatles broke up, and some famous people, such as Elvis Presley and Jimi Hendrix, died. This is when many new musicians started to become famous; Elton John was one (although he didn't get a number one single until 1990). There was also the shocking Sex Pistols (picture ⑤).

In 1979 Pink Floyd produced the smash hit 'Another Brick in the Wall Part II', featuring a schoolchildren chorus singing "we don't need no education". It caused an uproar among teachers.

In the late 1970s, ska and reggae became popular, thanks to the large Jamaican community in Britain.

The first of the outrageous stars was Alice Cooper. They were part of a musical scene called Hard Rock.

In Britain young people wanted to switch off from the depressing world of strikes, so they began listening to music and watching exciting performers. This was when David Bowie emerged from the gloom with his amazing make-up and clothes (picture ②).

Another way of trying to find something new was glitter. The 1970s have been called the 'Glitter Years'. People wore hot pants and sequins. The most famous artists were Gary Glitter and

◄ ② David Bowie as Ziggy Stardust.

Queen (picture ③) (whose song 'Bohemian Rhapsody' is part of music legend, see '1990s' section, page 39).

In the 1970s, discos became popular and music was written specially for them.

▼ ③ Queen, one of the world's most famous bands, was top of the pops.

In complete contrast, there were other people who developed a new kind of folk music called 'New Age'. People also started to become interested in music from other countries. This was called 'World Music'.

Clothes in the 1970s

Discos appeared in the early 1970s and the clothes to be seen in were wide 'kipper' ties, and shirts with big collars. Many clothes were made to look shiny.

In the 1970s people were travelling all over the world on holiday and brought back new ideas with them.

Punk fashion

Punk began in the mid-1970s as a revolt by a few young people against the world they lived in. Many of these people were out of work and had little money, so the clothes they wore matched this. They cut up old clothes from charity shops and gave them frayed edges. They wore black leather and old jeans. This shocked many people because it had never been seen before.

Punks wore Doc Martens boots – even girls. They used padlocks and chains as necklaces and put studs and pins in their eyebrows, cheeks, noses and lips.

Punks wore their hair spiked into a Mohican hairstyle (picture ④), using sugar and water solutions and even glue for stiffening their hair. It was coloured pink or green with food dyes. Black make-up was used on eyes and lips.

Some punks shaved their heads just to offend. The punks were always a small group and soon disappeared, but some part of their fashion, such as torn clothing, still remains.

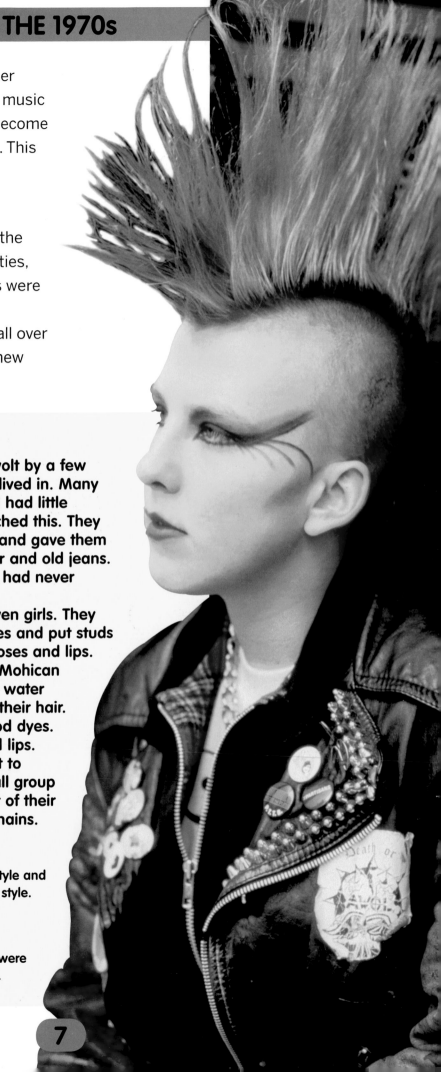

▶ ④ The 'Mohican' hairstyle and leathers were part of punk style.

◀ ⑤ The Sex Pistols were the biggest punk band.

Before the 1970s few homes had central heating, and shops and offices didn't have air conditioning. Few people travelled by car. But then all of these became common. As a result, people didn't have to use thick clothes to keep warm. Instead, they wore lighter weight clothes (as we do today) (picture ⑥).

▼▶ ⑥ The 'Swinging 60s' were over, but clothing styles continued to change, with bell-bottomed trousers, tightly fitting clothes and hair worn long. Bean bags were used as chairs by younger people and university students. One of the craze toys of the early 1970s was the rubber ball with handles called the Spacehopper. It was used by children to bounce about both indoors and outside.

Most striking was that people stopped wearing hats and long overcoats and went for shorter, waist-length coats with artificial fur collars.

Women's trouser suits became all the rage and platform heeled shoes rose up to 10 cm from the ground.

Then fashion changed again, this time to colour co-ordinated clothes, so that bottoms, tops and shoes could all be bought together. Many people started to wear chunky cardigans because they saw them in the TV series 'Starsky and Hutch'.

The Troubles

In one part of Britain – Northern Ireland – from 1969 until 1997, parts of the two main faith communities – the Protestants (Loyalist/Unionists) and the Catholics (Republican/Nationalists) – waged an undeclared war on one another.

This conflict had begun over 300 years earlier, when Northern Ireland had been settled by English and Scottish Protestants in what was, at that time, the entirely Roman Catholic island of Ireland. From then on, wars and conflicts raged from time to time. The two communities each felt unfairly treated. At the start of the 20th century the Catholic majority of Ireland formed an armed protest group called the IRA. Battles between the IRA and the British Army occurred and eventually Ireland was divided into the Republic of Ireland (an independent country) and Northern Ireland – Ulster – which stayed part of the United Kingdom.

This division did not result in peace in the north, where there was a Protestant majority. By the middle of the 1960s both the Catholics and Protestants were forming armed groups because each felt under threat from the other. The ongoing conflict was called 'the Troubles'. In 1972 nearly 500 people were killed and Northern Ireland was then ruled from London.

The Troubles mostly affected Northern Ireland, but bombings spread into the mainland too, as with the 1984 bombing of the Brighton hotel where the Conservative leaders were staying (picture ⑦).

Two events inflamed the Troubles more than any other. The first was in 1972 when a civil rights march ended disastrously with the shooting of some civilians on a day that became known as Bloody Sunday. Another moment of tragic violence occurred in August 1998 when a bomb in Omagh killed 29 people out shopping.

Eventually, some people on both sides made real political progress, leading to the Good Friday Agreement.

At the present time, all armed groups have ceased fighting and government is now shared between both communities, leading to real hope that the Troubles can be put behind everyone.

◀ (7) The collapsed front of the Brighton Grand Hotel after its bombing by the IRA in 1984.

Shopping and cooking in the 1970s

In the 1970s people began owning freezers, and cars became commonplace. The result was the 'weekly shop' to large stores and the terms 'hypermarket' and 'superstore' were used.

At the same time 'CONVENIENCE FOODS' began to be bought. People started to think that it was just fine to stop cooking and eat foods made in factories. All they needed was heating through.

For instance, people stopped boiling potatoes and instead used potato powder. "For mash get Smash" was one of the most famous adverts where alien characters laughed at the idea of digging up potatoes from the ground, peeling them, then cooking and mashing them (picture (8)). Smash adverts helped to make the idea of convenience foods seem modern.

▲▶ (8) The "For mash get Smash" aliens (right), and a modern packet of Smash (above).

▶ ⑨ **Takeaway containers came in during the 1970s.**

During the 1970s people ate less fruit and vegetables than ever before, even though it was the first time that fruit juice was sold in Britain.

People ate bigger portions of meat (about twice what most people would eat today). Hamburgers arrived from America, and people went to the new, trendy Wimpy bars.

By the 1970s there were over 1,000 Wimpy bars (which still served customers at their tables). However, McDonald's opened its first store in Britain in 1974 with counter service, new tastes and cheaper foods.

Chinese fish and chip shops began to sell Chinese takeaway food and Indian takeaways began to open across the country (picture ⑨).

In towns, the weekly shop was causing parking problems as people with heavy bags wanted to park next to where they bought their food. So the bigger stores built out of town centres with large car parks, something that the Americans had started to do in the 1950s.

Soon this caused shops in town centres to find trade reduce. The number of grocery stores fell from 150,000 in 1961 to 60,000 in 1981.

People spent about a quarter of their weekly wage on food, which had fallen from a third of their weekly wage in the 1950s. At the same time, people were earning more, so they could buy more food and still have money to spend on other things.

There was a trend to overseas holidays, and so people tasted foods from other countries and wanted to eat them here as well. This is when supermarkets started to sell yoghurt, extra-virgin olive oil, pizzas and many other overseas foods.

In the 1970s many children gave up eating school dinners and bought new-style snacks from shops.

What people, on average, ate each week in the 1970s:

2.6 litres of milk
4.5 eggs
340 g of cooking fat and oil
1,000 g of bread

Immigration

People have always come to settle in Britain from overseas. But in the 1970s the scale of this **IMMIGRATION** speeded up dramatically. People who had been born in Britain became nervous. They were frightened by what they did not understand and, in particular, by the speed with which it was happening. They did not know what effect this would bring to their jobs and so on. As a result, those arriving from Asia, Africa and the Caribbean, experienced prejudice that they never expected. Many of these people had always thought of Britain as their second home, so they, too, were frightened of what the future might hold.

In 1945, Britain's non-white residents were just a few thousand. By 1970 they had grown to 1.4 million – a third of whom had been born in Britain.

The biggest single period of immigration came in 1972 when the Ugandan dictator, General Idi Amin, expelled 80,000 African Asians from the country on purely racial grounds. Britain allowed 28,000 Ugandan Asians to arrive in two months.

New laws rushed in meant that British passport holders born overseas could only settle in Britain if they had a work permit and could prove that a parent or grandparent had been born in the UK.

People were confused. On the one hand in 1978 Viv Anderson became the first black footballer to be selected for the full England team and went on to win 30 caps (picture ⑩). He was a hero. Yet people also saw many black unemployed who said they did not feel part of the country.

Problems caused by immigration and prejudice were so great that in 1976 the government set up the Commission for Racial Equality.

◀ ⑩ **Black football stars began to emerge in the 1970s. This is Nottingham Forest's Viv Anderson.**

Being in a 1970s school

Secondary schools were now nearly all comprehensive. Many were in new buildings that had been built quickly using prefabricated methods. They looked like piles of boxes, often with coloured plastic panels. The first of them were already starting to leak because of shoddy workmanship and flawed design.

Desks had formica tops and chairs were all one piece, with seat and back made of plastic fixed to steel legs. But some classrooms now had carpet tiles instead of the wooden floors that had been the rule for nearly a century.

Some classrooms had a TV on a stand and even a video cassette recorder (VCR), so that schools' programmes could be recorded and played back (picture ⑫).

But while government money went into new secondary schools, primary children still had to work in old Victorian buildings and some still had outside toilets.

▼▶ ⑪ **In 1977 the first 'Star Wars' film was released (now re-titled 'Star Wars Episode IV: A New Hope'). Annuals, toys and Star Wars trading cards (complete with sticks of gum) were very collectable.**

▼ ⑫ **An old school video cassette recorder (VCR).**

▼ ⑬ The 'chopper' bike was very popular in the 1970s.

Toys and games

These all changed quickly because of the start of widespread television advertising. Just before Christmas manufacturers brought out the 'latest thing' to attract parents to buy it (pictures ⑪, ⑬ and ⑭), and last year's toy was thrown away. It was the start of the throw-away society.

The first computer game **CONSOLE** arrived in 1977 (see picture ⑮, page 16).

▶ ⑭ Over one million skateboards were bought during 1977.

15

▼ ⑮ Electronic games began selling fast in the late 1970s. The Video Computer System by Atari was first released in the UK in 1977. It was called the Atari 2600 and had a woodgrain console, plastic paddles, and rubber joysticks. You could play Tennis, Outlaw, Breakout and Space Wars – all games used cartridges. The 'Atari' went on to be very successful throughout the 1980s.

Atari 'paddles' for playing tennis.

Atari 'joysticks'.

Many Atari 2600 games were released in the 1980s.

Radio and television

This was the time of the comedy shows (many of which are still being shown as repeats). There were 'Are You Being Served?', 'Fawlty Towers', 'Porridge', 'Some Mothers Do 'Ave 'Em', 'Rising Damp', 'The Last of the Summer Wine and 'Monty Python's Flying Circus' (picture ⑯).

In the 1970s game shows were also increasing, and chat shows began.

▲▶ ⑯ Some popular 1970s TV shows had companion annuals, LPs and videos, and are still available today on DVD: (clockwise from top left) 'Some Mothers Do 'Ave 'Em'; 'Dad's Army'; 'Starsky and Hutch'; 'Fawlty Towers'; The Wombles (whose motto was to "make good use of bad rubbish"); 'Bionic Woman' starring Lindsay Wagner; and 'Tiswas', the popular Saturday morning children's programme with Chris Tarrant which ran from 1974 to 1982.

The 1980s

The 1980s started with strikes and wars and ended with DESIGNER CLOTHES. By 1989 the 'feel good factor' was back.

The first half of the 1980s was a time of terrible difficulty for Britain. There was a war and then strikes. However, in the second part of the decade, all was forgotten, as Britain surged ahead.

The Falklands War

In 1982, Argentina suddenly tried to take over the Falkland Islands in the South Atlantic Ocean which, by choice of its inhabitants, was a part of Britain. The government raced troops to the scene, ferrying them in cruise liners (picture ①). Britain won the struggle, and a great national pride surged over the country.

▲ ① The Falklands War was a major part of the early 1980s, with Britain having to supply its troops to almost the other side of the world. Actual casualties were remarkably light.

1980s timeline

1980
John Lennon assassinated.
Mount St Helens erupts.
Plastic milk bottles appear in supermarkets.
Post-it notes invented.

1981
Prince Charles and Lady Diana Spencer's wedding.
New plague identified as AIDS.
The personal computer (PC) introduced by IBM.
First space shuttle launched.
First London Marathon held.

1982
'ET' movie.
Falkland Islands invaded by Argentina.

1983
CDs and camcorders arrive on the market.
First British breakfast time television programme.
The one pound coin introduced.

1984
Beginning of the miners' strike.
IRA bomb goes off in Brighton hotel where Conservative leaders were staying.
Band Aid started with the song, 'Do they know it's Christmas?'

1980　　1981　　1982　　1983　　1984

The power struggle at home

The 1970s had been a difficult decade in Britain. It was a time when there were strikes, and the trade unions played a large part in saying how the country should be run. Britain was making shoddy goods and people were not buying them. Prices and wages were rising out of control (called inflation).

At the end of the 1970s, the problems of strikes and unions caused the Labour Party to collapse. The Conservative Party, led by Margaret Thatcher (picture ②), came to power saying that they would make a stand against the unions. There were some terrible battles, but in the end the government won.

The miners' strike

During the 1980s an event took place which has shaped the way we live today. It all centred around the coal miners, whose union was the National Union of Miners (NUM) led by Arthur Scargill. At that time the unions in Britain were very powerful. They had even brought down the government twice in the 1970s. The new Conservative government began a programme of closing what they thought were unprofitable coal mines. The union, fearing that many of their members would lose their jobs, thought it was powerful enough to stop this. The government, led by Margaret Thatcher, refused to back down.

In 1984 the miners went on strike. The government fought against them, bringing in non-union workers. There were many battles between union and police.

The strike lasted many months, but it was not given support by most other unions. Later on, some miners split from the NUM and went back to work. Eventually the NUM had to go back too.

The failure of the miners' leaders to win a political battle meant an end to the power of the unions to bring down governments. It also led to the Labour Party changing its beliefs and becoming 'New Labour', as we see it today.

As a result of the actions, the government set about building power stations that did not use coal, and coal mining in Britain became less and less important.

◀ ② Prime Minister Margaret Thatcher wearing a power suit. Her hair was puffed out using the new mousse and gel materials popular at the time.

1985	1986	1987	1988	1989
First British mobile phone call is made.	Chernobyl nuclear accident. USSR launches Mir space station.	DNA first used to convict criminals. Black Monday – world stock exchanges collapse. Hurricane force winds sweep southern England. World population 5 billion.	Pan Am Flight 103 bombed over Lockerbie, Scotland.	Berlin Wall falls. Cold War ends.

Weblink: www.CurriculumVisions.com

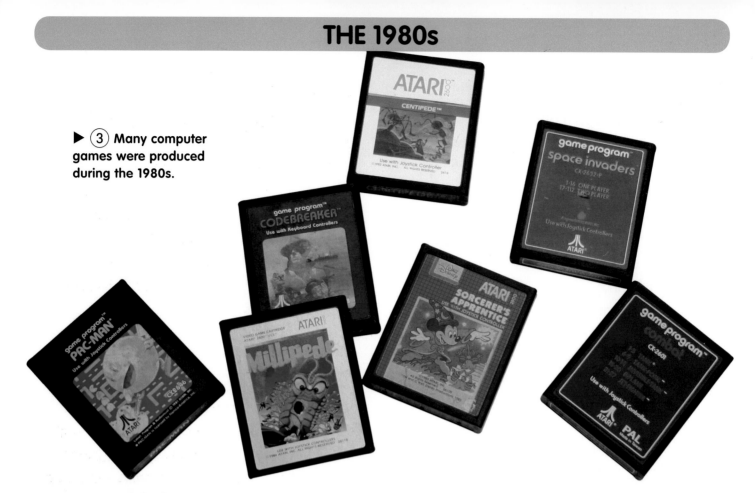

▶ ③ Many computer games were produced during the 1980s.

New wealth for some

After the end of the battle between unions and government, the face of Britain changed. Prices no longer rose by 25% a year but steadied. The quality of what Britain made went up and more people in the world wanted to buy it.

It was the end of an era, not just because of the strikes, but because the world was changing fast. People in Britain had to face the fact that they could no longer rely on the old ways of earning a living. People in China and India were making goods cheaper than people in Britain (because their wages were much lower). So many factories making traditional goods, such as clothing, closed and people had to find new kinds of work. This caused many jobs to be lost, especially in the older industrial areas, such as lowland Scotland, northern England and South Wales.

In the 1980s more money was made from insurance and banking than by making cars. The new growth was therefore not in making things in factories, but in trading in offices. The greatest growth was in the City of London. The amounts of money that some people made were spectacular.

This was also the start of the computer age and companies designing computer games, and other things to do with electronics, grew quickly (picture ③).

Cold War ends

Hugely important events occurred in the 1980s. The Soviet Union (which included Russia and countries such as Poland) started to fall apart because they were running out of money. Many Eastern European countries wanted to buy western things. They started to make their governments break away from the Soviet Union. One of the most famous of these was the breakaway of Poland.

Environment

The 1980s was a time when people started to become more aware of the way they were affecting the environment. This was highlighted when, in 1986, the core of a Soviet nuclear power station at Chernobyl melted and radioactive materials were released into the air. It was the first global environmental disaster.

One further immensely important thing happened. Since the 1950s, the Soviet Union and Western Countries had pointed nuclear weapons at each other. It was a time called the **COLD WAR**. No shots were actually fired, but the weapons made the world a very dangerous place.

As the Soviet Union weakened towards the end of the 1980s it finally agreed to stop building more and more weapons (the Soviet Union had simply run out of money) and the Cold War ended.

Living on credit

Despite Chernobyl, the environment was not such an important issue as it is today. Instead people were determined to have a good time and spend, spend, spend.

Credit cards became widespread and people in Britain began spending money just to keep up the image of being successful. Many people borrowed the money to do this using their new credit cards. It was called 'Living on Credit'.

Shopping malls

Shopping began to change in Britain in the 1980s. Because more people had cars, they were able to go to new, larger shopping areas built near to main roads and especially motorway junctions. These were called out-of-town shopping malls and they had vast car parks. These were not hypermarkets selling food, but stores selling clothes and electrical goods.

As wealthier people went to these centres, so they stopped going to local stores and, as a result, the centres of many British cities started to see even fewer shoppers. Many stores did not have enough business to keep going and they began to close. So, in the 1980s, a difference grew up between where the better off and less well off shopped. The gap between the better off and less well off widened.

Yuppies and dinkies

The 1980s was a time when middle class professional people started to group themselves by initials. The new wealthy classes were called Dinky ('Double Income No Kids Yet'). There were Empty Nesters (married couples whose children had grown up and moved out), Yuppies (Young Urban Professionals) and Woopies (Well Off Older People). There was even a name for their children: Tweenies (between 5 and 12 years old).

21

Fashion in the 1980s

In the 1980s, fashion designers were less interested in teenagers and they focused on people in their twenties who had good jobs and lots of money to spend.

This was the time when working business women in particular, took to 'power dressing' (see also page 19), meaning a dark suit with wide, padded shoulders (picture ④). The idea was that it showed the world that women were just as able to climb the success ladder as men. Successful women with this style were important characters in 'Dallas' (a TV programme, see page 27). Prime Minister Margaret Thatcher and Diana, Princess of Wales, both wore power suits. The style caught on.

▼ ④ In the 1980s there was a curious mixture of styles, as women dressed more like men while at work, and men dressed more like slobs when at home. Trainers became fashionable. It was still the time of the cassette.

New hair-setting materials – mousse and gel – were invented and women started to wear 'plumped up' hair.

As people tried to show 'they had arrived', they added accessories. No one who was anyone in the 1980s would have been seen without their Filofax (picture ⑤). It was a simple ringbinder that was small enough to go into a handbag or coat pocket. You kept your addresses, contacts, diary and much more in it. You could even get novels that fitted into a Filofax, so you could read it on the train (making sure everyone saw you had it, of course).

While suits were worn in the office, at home men and women started to wear track suits and trainers. People showed how wealthy they were by wearing designer trainers. In this way, the 1980s was the start of the designer age. It was trendy to be seen wearing the right brand, whether it was sportswear, perfumes, electrical equipment, cars, clothing, bags, luggage, scarves or even spectacles.

▲ ⑤ A Filofax.

What people, on average, ate each week in the 1980s:

2.4 litres of milk
3.7 eggs
320 g of cooking fat and oil
950 g of bread

Food and eating

With more money, and more kinds of food in the shops, some middle class people started taking cooking ideas from the new TV chefs. Madhur Jaffrey was a popular chef of the time, showing people how to cook Asian food.

But for many others it was the time when people stopped cooking altogether and purchased 'fast-foods' such as hamburgers and fries or convenience, ready-cooked frozen meals that simply needed reheating. This was because, in the 1980s, more mums than ever went to work and fewer families ate their meals together. In the 1980s the first chilled meals were introduced by Marks & Spencer. These were unfrozen, and only needed reheating. They kept a better flavour than frozen foods.

The age of personal computers

The 1980s was important for the introduction of the PC (picture ⑥).

A personal computer (PC) is usually a microcomputer whose price, size and capabilities make it suitable for personal usage. The term was popularised by Apple Computer with the Apple II in the late-1970s and early-1980s, and afterwards by IBM with the IBM PC.

Personal computers had been around before this, but they were expensive and did not do very much. In the 1980s new fast chips (for their time) were made. The world's biggest computer maker, IBM, decided to make a personal computer (PC) in 1981. At this time the chip ran at just under 5 MHz (they are typically 500 times faster today). At that time the floppy disk was also introduced.

Great strides were made in writing the programs to make the computers do more. The most successful software turned out to be the one called MS-DOS, bought from a small computer company and then developed by Microsoft led by Bill Gates.

▶ ⑥ A Commodore VIC20 far right, and an early Macintosh computer right.

In Britain, Alan Sugar started to make his fortune by selling the Amstrad range of computers.

All of these changes meant that, in the 1980s, a price war developed and people could at last afford computers at home. But they were still difficult to use because no one had made a 'click and point' mouse way of working. Then in the late 1980s came the first Apple home computers. In 1984 Steve Jobs at Apple introduced Macintosh with its user-friendly mouse (see picture below left).

Microwave ovens went on sale in the 1980s. They speeded up cooking times, and meant that whole meals could be ready in minutes.

With more demand for overseas foods, supermarket shelves bulged. Sainsbury's product range rose from 7,000 in 1980 to 17,000 in 1993.

During the 1980s the big food stores became bigger. The half a dozen biggest chains were now the places where over half the population shopped.

With traditional bakers losing business to the supermarkets, those in city centres changed to selling ready made sandwiches, pasties and other convenience foods for office workers to buy during their lunch break.

Changes in families

In the 1980s more people than ever lived on their own. The number of one parent families grew while many older women were living on their own simply because women generally live longer than men.

People were also marrying later and having fewer children. The classic advert of the 1980s that showed this change was run by Gold Blend Instant Coffee. It showed two single people in their 30s, each living in their own apartment. Gold Blend was dearer than many other types of coffee, and showing successful people with products meant that more expensive items could be sold because those in work were earning more than ever before. However, in the 1980s more people were also unemployed – another reason why the gap between rich and poor widened.

Toys and games

Many of the toys that had been popular in previous years were still selling well in the 1980s, but this was the time when computer games were sold in large numbers. For example, Game Boy was launched in 1989 (in black and white) (picture ⑦).

Some 'must have' toys of the 1980s were the Cabbage Patch dolls – each with their own unique faces (picture ⑧) – and the Rubik's cube puzzle (picture ⑨).

▲▼ ⑦ An original 1989 Game Boy with game cartridges.

▲ ⑧ The Cabbage Patch doll was the doll fad of the 1980s.

▼ ⑨ Over 100 million Rubik's cubes were sold between 1980–1982.

▲ ⑩ The cast of 'Dallas', the American soap launched in 1980.

Television in the 1980s

Breakfast TV was introduced in the UK in 1983.

In 1985 the BBC launched 'EastEnders', with its mix of less prosperous people as a southern rival to northern 'Coronation Street'.

British TV started to show American soap operas such as 'Dallas' and 'Dynasty' (about wealthy people). In 1980 'Dallas' was the most popular TV series in the world (picture ⑩).

Weblink: www.CurriculumVisions.com

In the 1980s film and TV producers started to spend more and more money to give the thrills that the audience wanted. 'Miami Vice', for example, cost a million pounds each episode. Blockbuster movies were to cost hundreds of millions of pounds.

VCRs (video recorders) were now found in most homes and people started to record their TV programmes, or play those they could hire. This was also the decade when remote controls were added to TVs and other equipment. Before this you had to get up to press the buttons on the set.

Satellites

Almost without anyone noticing, the 1980s became the first decade when stationary satellites were in place around the world. Using these satellites, it was possible to beam live events around the world.

Meanwhile, cable and satellite networks were being established, and the 'box' in the living room (and the ones in the bedrooms and the kitchen!) became the main source of our entertainment.

Music of the 1980s

During the 1980s new radio stations came on air and music was everywhere (picture ⑪). MTV, the music video channel, was launched in the United States in the summer of 1981. This meant that musicians could be seen, as well as heard, performing their latest music.

Madonna, Michael Jackson, Prince, George Michael and many others produced videos just to sell records.

There were many new bands, but it was the new ideas of Heavy Metal and the New Romantic style of dressing up outrageously

▲▶ ⑪ Pop stars and politics suddenly mixed when, in 1984, singers Bob Geldof and Midge Ure organised help for starving people in Ethiopia. Britain's top music stars joined together to form Band Aid, producing a single 'Do they know it's Christmas?'. This was followed on 13 July 1985 by the Live Aid concert. It was shown worldwide due to the new satellite technology.

that caught everyone's attention. Artists famous for this included Spandau Ballet, Adam & The Ants, Culture Club, David Bowie and Duran Duran.

Immigration

By 1981 Britain had riots on its city streets. They were largely sparked by racial issues. In Brixton, for example, where many Afro-Caribbean people had settled, young people rioted because they said they were being unfairly targeted by the police.

But more immigrants were gaining a better position in Britain. In 1987 four non-white politicians were elected MPs.

Immigration patterns were changing in the 1980s. During the 1980s, the majority of black immigrants coming into Britain were not from the Caribbean, but directly from Africa: from Nigeria and Ghana in West Africa, Somalia and Kenya in East Africa and Zimbabwe and South Africa in Southern Africa.

A large number of people from Asia continued to arrive, as they had since the 1950s. Pakistanis had been recruited to work on the railways. Punjabis went to work in the steel works of the Midlands and in the area surrounding London's Heathrow airport. They also went to textile areas such as Leicester and the North. British Bangladeshis went to London's East End.

By this time, many people of Asian and African descent were British born. But the communities in which they grew up were quite closed and self-contained. Integration between the new 'black British' and the majority was not happening.

Also, in the 1980s, it was already clear that many people of Asian and African descent were successful at business. Some black people and some white people resented this. It was an unsettled time.

The 1990s

During this decade many people in Britain became better off and spent more time than ever on overseas holidays or buying apartments abroad. Supermarket chains replaced many small shops.

The 1990s saw huge change. Some of the change was worldwide, for example, the rise of the Internet, making it possible for more people to explore the world, and to contribute to it. It allowed some to work from home rather than in an office.

Some of it was Europe wide, for example, the fall of the Soviet Union, and some of it was entirely British, such as the Good Friday Agreement that would lead to the end of the Troubles in Northern Ireland (see page 10).

It was also the time in which New Labour came to power. This was the first Labour government for nearly 20 years and it promised to be more forward-looking, and less attached to the unions than any Labour government before it.

The Global Village

During the 1990s, the world shrank. Cheap airline flights made it possible to fly anywhere in the world more affordably than ever before. In the 1990s no one really understood the way this might affect global warming. There was also a rapid growth in cruise shipping, and huge liners were built to allow thousands at a time to visit places across the world (picture ①).

Flying also meant that fresh goods could be sent to Britain from all over the world. As a result, large parts of the world, and especially poorer countries, made a living by sending fresh food to Britain for the first time. People stopped thinking about seasonal foods because they could be grown somewhere at any time of the year and then just flown in.

1990s timeline

Ban on British beef because of the BSE scare. Hundreds of thousands of animals were slaughtered to try to curb it.

The Internet grows explosively from now on as the World Wide Web is created.

Women priests allowed in the Church of England.
Channel Tunnel opens, connecting Britain and France and Eurostar goes direct to Paris.
The Provisional IRA declares a ceasefire.
National Lottery begins.

1990   **1991**   **1992**   **1993**   **1994**

The Soviet Union collapses leaving the country we now call Russia. The Gulf War begins following Iraq's invasion of Kuwait. A coalition of 30 countries, including the US and Britain went off to fight, but in the end Saddam Hussein kept control of most of Iraq. It would all come back to haunt Britain and America in 2003.

Teenager Stephen Lawrence killed 22 April. London's Bishopsgate bombing 24 April by IRA. Agreement signed between the UK and Irish governments on the future of Northern Ireland.

By the end of the 1990s, there was actually less need to go out of your home at all, because shopping channels arrived on UK TV due to Freeview, cable and satellite services.

▲ ① Cheap fare airlines and cruise ships opened up the world to many low-budget tourists.

▶ ② There was widespread mourning after the sudden death in a car crash of Diana, Princess of Wales, on 31 August 1997.

Swaminarayan Hindu Temple opens in Neasden and is the largest in Europe.
Alison Hargreaves is the first woman to climb Mount Everest without oxygen or sherpas.
13 December – Riots in Brixton.

'Harry Potter and the philosopher's stone' is published.
New Labour takes over from the Conservatives.
Hong Kong returned to China.
August 31 – Death of Diana, Princess of Wales (picture ②).
Referendum in Scotland and Wales for devolution.

1995   **1996**   **1997**   **1998**   **1999**

First genetically modified foods sold in the UK.
IRA bomb explodes in Manchester city centre.
5 July – Dolly the cloned sheep is born.
The Spice Girls release their first record.

Good Friday Peace Agreement in Northern Ireland.
Omagh bombing kills 29 in Northern Ireland.
Human Rights Act becomes law.

Minimum wage introduced.
The Euro becomes the new European currency.
London Eye and Millennium Dome built.

Fashion in the 90s

In the 90s people tried to look more casual (picture ③). Those leading the way adopted grunge.

At the start of the 1990s people were still wearing slim stone-washed jeans, but then the fashion swung to relaxed hip hop fit widepants fashion. Trousers were now worn by everyone.

In secondary schools, loose cargo pants and fitness sportswear were often a general uniform. The 1990s also saw the arrival of the 'fleece'.

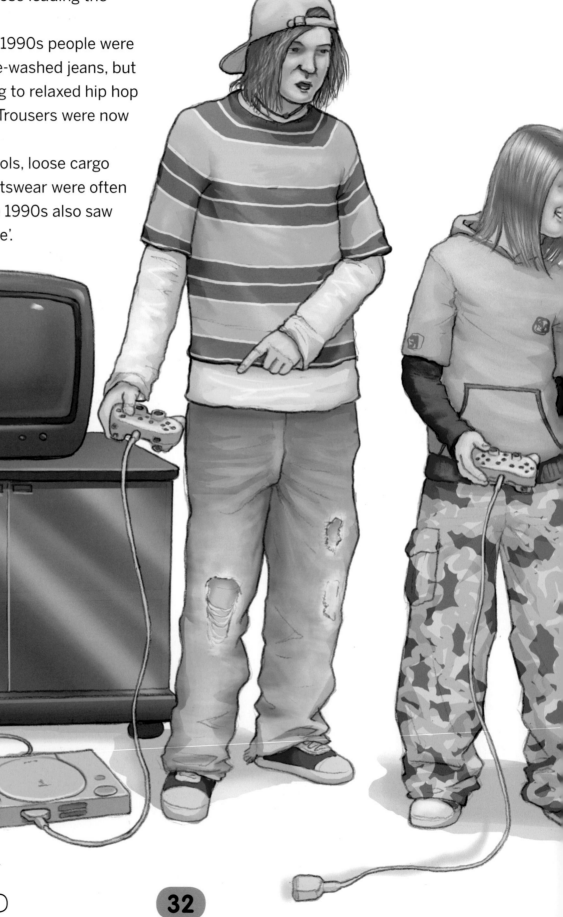

Girls had their hair straight and hanging down.

In offices, old rules about wearing jackets and ties were often done away with.

Hooded sweat-shirts came in and some teenage boys developed the 'hoodie' look.

At the same time, as fashion became so easy to see on the Internet, people all over the world began to dress remarkably alike.

◀ ③ Here you can see the way that everyone was dressing down. Jeans no longer fitted, but had to look worn out and baggy. Many people wore trainers all the time. Over and undershirts were common, as were fleeces of various kinds.

This was the age when computer games, using interactive consoles, became all the rage, prompting doctors to worry about the health of people who gave up games and even going outdoors in favour of virtual reality.

Weblink: www.CurriculumVisions.com

Mobile phones

During the 1990s the Filofax was replaced with laptops and electronic organisers. But the real must-have of the 1990s was a mobile phone.

The first phone call using a real mobile phone was made as recently as 1978 and the first network was not licensed until 1983. Then it took a long time to set up the aerials needed to run networks, and the early mobile phones were very large – about the size of a brick – and just as heavy and very expensive (picture ④). Nearly all were designed for use in cars and were thus called car-phones.

The first truly portable phones, using digital signals, were not introduced until 1990, only about 20 years ago. It was also at this time that mobile phones shrank in size and weight, so that 100–200 g phones became common.

The first network using digital signals was set up in Finland, which then became a leader in phone technology (for example, Nokia). However, mobile phones were rapidly taken up by Britain, through companies such as Vodaphone. Around 90% of the world's population now has mobile phone coverage, so that people in Britain can now reach almost anyone in the world.

By the end of the 1990s, mobile phones had become so common, some researchers believed there were more mobile phones than people in Britain.

They gave the chance for people to chat or text, and the mobile phone companies were able to get back the money they had invested in the phone towers, satellites and so on.

About half of all children now have mobile phones. Many children get cheap use of phones through texting.

What people, on average, ate each week in the 1990s:

1.941 litres of milk (0.709 litres of which was skimmed or semi-skimmed milk)
3.1 eggs
225 g of cooking fat and oil
850 g of bread

▲ ⑤ Curry made up a quarter of all frozen convenience meals bought.

Food and eating

In the 1990s food got cheaper in real terms. At the end of the 1990s, an average home spent less on food than in the 1970s. Middle classes were earning more, and so they had more money to spend on other things (picture ⑥). Many people bought wine to drink with their meals. By the end of the 1990s on average families spent a sixth of their household spending on alcohol.

People bought less raw and frozen food in the 1990s. But sales of the new (more expensive) chilled foods went up. So, during the 1990s wealthier people turned to chilled ready meals bought from supermarkets. But it was different for the poor. At the end of the 1990s, average spending on food by the poorest people was £26 a week, (it was £111 a week for the wealthier). Poor people also tended to buy the least healthy foods and buy more cooked meals from fast-food restaurants, even though healthy foods are cheaper.

Changing tastes

Indian food became more and more popular, not just to buy out, but to cook at home (picture ⑤). Chicken Tikka Masala was Britain's most popular national restaurant dish by the end of the 1990s. More than a quarter of chilled meals were Italian and about a quarter Indian, but British meals were less than a fifth.

▼ ⑥ Pizza was a classic home delivery meal of the 1990s.

◀ ④ A mobile from the 1980s!

The Internet

The Internet became part of many people's lives in the 1990s, with most businesses having to have a web page and an email address. Because everyone could join for little money, vast amounts of information was 'published' on the web for others to see. But it all started nearly 40 years earlier as part of the space race.

In 1957 the then USSR launched Sputnik, the first artificial earth satellite.

In 1962 the US Air Force made a study of how it could keep control of its missiles and bombers, after a nuclear attack. It was told that it would need a network of command stations, so that if one were hit all the rest could continue. They decided that the best way to do this was to send information in tiny electronic 'packets' each with an electronic address attached to it. Each packet was sent from one computer to another until it arrived at its destination. Here it was joined up with all of the other packets and could then be read.

In 1969 four experimental centres were connected by telephone lines. Each centre was called a host. Hosts called

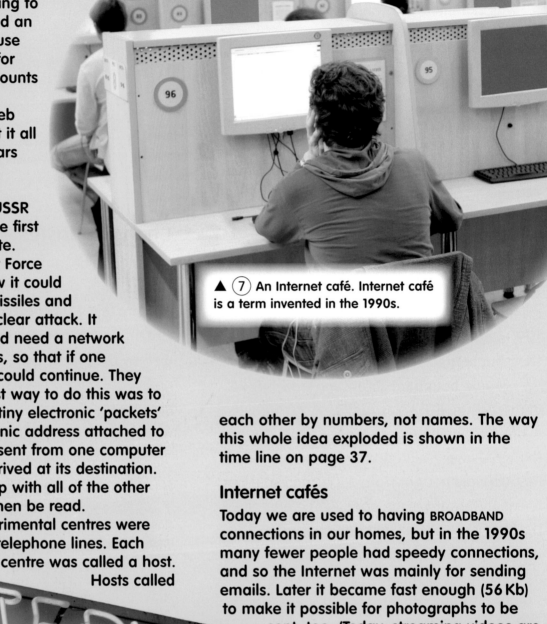

▲ ⑦ An Internet café. Internet café is a term invented in the 1990s.

each other by numbers, not names. The way this whole idea exploded is shown in the time line on page 37.

Internet cafés

Today we are used to having BROADBAND connections in our homes, but in the 1990s many fewer people had speedy connections, and so the Internet was mainly for sending emails. Later it became fast enough (56 Kb) to make it possible for photographs to be sent, too. (Today, streaming videos are common, but they need many Mb of bandwidth and that did not happen until the middle of the 2000s).

In the 1980s personal computers were very expensive. By the 1990s they had become cheaper, but were still out of many people's reach. So, in 1994, the idea of a Cybercafé was invented in London. Here, banks of computers were arranged in a shop (the café) and rented

▼ ⑧ A person using a laptop in a Wireless Hot Spot, in this case an airport lounge.

out to people who just came in off the street. Often a terminal was rented by the minute. Later, with the development of the Internet, the name Cybercafé was replaced with Internet Café (picture ⑦).

Internet Wireless Hot Spots

Internet cafés are still popular in poorer parts of the world, but in Britain, the Internet café's main role gradually changed to being a place where people travelling could connect to family and friends.

By the beginning of the 2000s, business people found Internet cafés inconvenient and wanted to use their own laptops. The idea of wireless connection was also catching on. So many public places and hotels now have Wireless Hot Spots, where people with wireless-enabled computers can simply sit wherever they want and connect in private (picture ⑧). The new generation of mobile phones can do the same job.

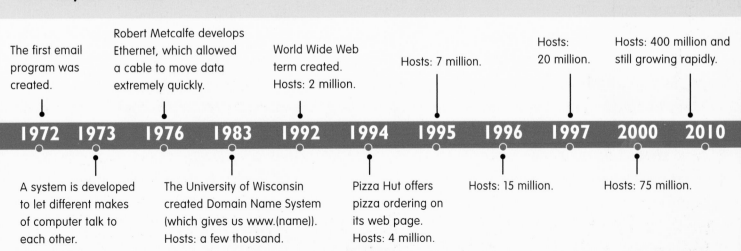

The first email program was created.

Robert Metcalfe develops Ethernet, which allowed a cable to move data extremely quickly.

World Wide Web term created.
Hosts: 2 million.

Hosts: 7 million.

Hosts: 20 million.

Hosts: 400 million and still growing rapidly.

1972   1973   1976   1983   1992   1994   1995   1996   1997   2000   2010

A system is developed to let different makes of computer talk to each other.

The University of Wisconsin created Domain Name System (which gives us www.(name)).
Hosts: a few thousand.

Pizza Hut offers pizza ordering on its web page.
Hosts: 4 million.

Hosts: 15 million.

Hosts: 75 million.

37

Shops

Superstores got bigger and bigger, but the number of local convenience stores also grew. These survived because they were open for long hours and sold a wide range of food, sweets and drinks. Many of them operated from converted petrol stations. To capture this market as well, the large supermarket chains began to buy up petrol station sites and convert them to their own brand convenience stores and filling stations.

To all of these were added discount chains, such as Aldi, Netto and Lidl, using large warehouses and selling at rock-bottom prices.

Eating habits

Meals were taking shorter and shorter times to prepare. This was because people cooking at home were buying foods that were faster to cook, such as pasta and rice, and leaner cuts of meat. So whereas 50 years before, people would cook a stew for hours in order to tenderise a cheap cut of meat, stir-frying a wafer-thin steak took less than a minute.

During the 1990s more people rushed to work and school without eating breakfast, or ate a snack while travelling. Many people just ate a snack for lunch too. This was good news for fast-food shops and many new ones opened including many famous chains from the United States, such as Subway.

Weight watching

The 1990s were a time when people started to notice that they were too heavy to be healthy. However, they didn't do too much about it.

Curiously, by the 1990s there was less fat in foods, so the number of calories people ate a day was, on average, just 1,900 – much lower than the 2,500 of the 1970s. However, people did less exercise at play or at work (going to school by car instead of walking, and so on), so the number of calories they needed also went down. The result was fatter people because many were simply not burning the calories off.

Music of the 1990s

In the 1980s singles were still sold on 'vinyl'. But the days of measuring success by the number of singles sold was over. By 1990 the first number one single of the year sold only 28,000 copies. It was by the boy band New Kids on the Block.

◄ ⑨ CDs by Blur and the Spice Girls. The Spice Girls sold 55 million records.

▶ ⑩ Rollerblades were very popular in the 1990s. They were roller skates with their wheels lined up in single file.

The lack of single sales did not stop many singers becoming wealthy and famous: Kylie Minogue, Madonna and Elton John among them. Cliff Richard had his 100th top 40 hit and became the only person to have a number 1 in the 1950s, 60s, 70s, 80s and 90s.

Queen re-released their song Bohemian Rhapsody which became a number one single (it had originally been on their 1975 album).

Yet alongside the national artists, music was now splitting up into regions. This was called the Indie music scene, with groups specialising in playing in just one part of the country.

By the middle of the 1990s something new had emerged in Britain. It was known as Britpop – a mixture of British rock and roll over the previous 30 years. Famous bands included Blur, Suede and Oasis and of the girl bands, the most famous were the Spice Girls (picture ⑨).

39

Television

The most important event of the 1990s was the change to satellite TV. Before the end of the 1980s everyone had just a small number of channels – BBC1 and 2, ITV and Channel 4. Then, in 1990, Sky was launched as a satellite broadcast. As the years went by, this would lead the way to Britain receiving hundreds of channels, both from the UK and overseas.

By 1994 the National Lottery was being shown on TV. There were new types of comedy, too, the most famous being 'Absolutely Fabulous'. By 1998 new game shows had appeared, headed by 'Who Wants to be a Millionaire?' (picture ⑪).

▲ ⑪ 'Who Wants to be a Millionaire?' electronic board game was one of the UK's top selling toys by the end of the 1990s.

◄◄► ⑫ Pokémon video games were second in popularity only to Super Mario. Children could collect miniature models of the 'pocket monsters' as well as the Pokémon trading cards game.

Toys

Perhaps the best known toys of the 1990s were Tinkywinky, Dipsy, Lala and Po – the Teletubbies. They were started as a BBC TV show. The Teletubbies spoke in a gurgling baby language similar to its target audience. But it immediately produced a demand for soft cuddly toys (picture ⑬). While for older children the Furby became the must-have toy, along with a pair of rollerblades (picture ⑭ and picture ⑩, page 39).

But now there was a new level of computer game (picture ⑫). In the 1990s Super Mario Bros (Nintendo) with its challenge of saving the princess, became the biggest selling game of all time.

▲ ⑬ Teletubbies were a completely new form of toy that started out as a TV show, rather as Thunderbirds had in the 1970s. Above are three of the four Teletubbies: Tinkywinky (purple), Lala (yellow) and Po (red).

◄ ⑭ Furby was an interactive furry toy with a mind of its own. It spoke its own language and talked with other Furby toys.

Weblink: www.CurriculumVisions.com

The 21st century

In the first years of the 21st century, security, immigration and the soaring price of food and energy have been on most people's minds.

▶ ① **The London Eye during the celebrations to welcome in the new millennium.**

As people all over the country watched firework displays to welcome in the new millennium (picture ①), they could hardly have foreseen the dramatic way their lives would change in the years just after.

There was a lot to be pleased about: most people were wealthier than ever before and most people had jobs. New features such as the Internet were exciting with a great surge in Internet shopping and banking.

People could order online and just wait for their goods to be delivered.

But people were also worrying. They worried, for example, about their carbon footprint. Until the 2000s no one would have known what this was, but it was becoming clear that our increasing use of energy was causing global warming and we would have to do something about it, by wasting less and being more efficient. People overseas were

▶ ② The destruction of New York's World Trade Center by terrorists in 2001 was an event that changed the lives of the world – many British lives were lost in this act of terrorism.

becoming wealthier too, and they wanted energy. So the price of gas, electricity and petrol began to rise and rise. The same people were wealthy enough to eat meat rather than just vegetables, and sixty million extra people were being added to the world each year. All of that has produced food shortages and put prices up.

The terrorist threat

Then, on 11 September 2001, an event happened that changed the world instantly. A very tiny number of terrorists (often loosely grouped as belonging to 'Al-Qaeda'), succeeded in flying two planes into the twin towers of the World Trade Center in New York (picture ②). This became known as 9–11. Although it occurred in the United States, the suicide bombing had immediate effects on Britain, as well as the rest of the world. Yet despite much tighter security (picture ③), our own catastrophe occurred with the 7 July 2005 suicide underground and bus bombings in London (now called 7–7).

Attempts to stop further terrorist attacks haunt much of our daily lives even today.

▼ ③ People entering and leaving airports and many other kinds of public building now expect body and luggage searches.

Weblink: www.CurriculumVisions.com

Immigration

Between 1991 and 2001, the British population grew by 2.2 million. Half of this was due to people arriving from abroad. By 2001, 4.3 million people living in Britain (about 7.5% of the country) were born abroad (nearly double the number of 1971).

Most people recently arriving from overseas live in London and nearly 1.7 million foreign-born people now live in London, getting on for a quarter of the city population. In some areas it is much higher: in Wembley 52% were born abroad.

By 2000 there were about 2.3 million British Asians, making up 4% of the population of the United Kingdom. British Asians made up 50% of the UK's non-white population.

Then, in 2004, ten eastern European countries were made members of the European Union (picture ④). They were allowed to live and work anywhere they wanted, and between 2004 and 2006, about 2 million arrived – the majority from Poland.

But there was also a growth in asylum seekers. Between 1998 and 2000, 45,000 people arrived from Africa, 23,000 from the Indian sub-continent, 25,000 from other parts of Asia and 12,000 from the Americas.

As a result of immigration, longer lives and more babies being born, in 2009 the population had reached 61 million, and is forecast to reach 70 million by 2030.

▶ ④ The European Union was enlarged to 27 member states, so that it now covers most of Europe.

▶ ⑤ Organic food has increased in popularity.

The large population and huge immigration have worried people already living here. They don't know what changes the extra number of people will bring, and with worry comes tension between communities.

Global eating

In the 1990s we ate much food from overseas. Now food makers are making what they call 'home meal replacements'. You can see this by looking at the adverts on the TV or walking along the ready meal shelves of any large supermarket chain. This is because there is more money to be made in selling prepared food than by just selling the ingredients.

On the other hand, there is more and more sign that people want to eat healthily. Organic food is still a small part of what we buy, but it is increasing (picture ⑤). Many people now buy wholegrain (brown) bread instead of white because it has more fibre and is more healthy.

Crunch and catastrophe

In 2007 it was already clear that many Western countries were living on credit (borrowed from savers in the Middle and Far Eastern countries) rather than earning what they spent. Banks were also lending too easily to people who would never be able to pay back their house loans. It was a time when money was too cheap. House prices grew too fast. People were

What people, on average, ate each week in the 2000s:

1.8 litres of milk (1.1 litres of which was skimmed or semi-skimmed milk)
1.9 eggs
186 g of cooking fat and oil
800 g of bread
89 g of cakes and pastries
67 g of flour
567 g of fruit (226 g of apples and pears) 206 g of bananas

relying on prices that would never stay at such high levels. It was like a house of cards waiting to collapse. And it did. Suddenly, starting in August 2007, banks wanted their money back. But they couldn't get it. People started to worry about their savings kept in banks. Banks stopped lending money. Some banks were in danger of failing and the government had to support them. It all caused people to stop spending and so they bought less and goods could not be sold. This caused firms to put people out of work. In 2010 it still looked like a long haul before Britain (and the rest of the world) would get wealthy again.

The 1950s and today

So what has changed in Britain over the last sixty years? In 1950 people were still living with rationing, which meant that each person got just a small amount of a very limited variety of foods. At the time of Elizabeth II's coronation in 1953 the main celebration was that the government allowed everyone to get an extra 1lb (500 g) of sugar and 4 oz (150 g) of margarine!

It might seem as though everyone is eating rice and pasta if you go by the adverts, but we still eat quite small amounts of these, compared to chips, boiled potatoes and bread. Interestingly, we still eat the same range of foods as in the 1950s – bread, milk, meat and potatoes – but in different forms. In the 1950s families sat down to a dinner and ate roast beef and Yorkshire pudding with roast potatoes and cabbage. Now people might not eat together at all, but instead each person may heat up their own ready meal, or buy a burger at a local fast-food restaurant. We might reheat oven chips instead of cooking them for ourselves.

In the 1950s everyone ate butter. Today it is only a small part of the shelves dominated by 'healthy eating' spreads.

As fish has become over-caught and prices have risen, so we eat less fish than we did in the 1950s. In the 1950s we drank whole milk. Today we drink less milk than we did then, and most people drink semi-skimmed milk or skimmed milk. Hardly anyone ate yoghurt in the 1950s, but it is a common breakfast choice today.

We now eat less than half the number of eggs we ate in the mid-1950s. We eat far less red meat (lamb, pork, beef) and more white meat (chicken, turkey) than in the past.

We buy half the fats and oils we used in the 1950s, although much of the fat we eat is 'hidden' in cakes, processed foods and so on. The same is true of sugar. We now eat less sugar directly than people did under rationing in the Second World War, but we still eat more sugar than we think. A can of tinned soup, for example, may have the equivalent of 5 teaspoons of sugar in it.

In the 1950s, people would buy flour and make cakes and puddings. Now they buy them. As a result, the amount of flour we buy has halved.

Health

We are now expecting to live almost ten years more than people in the 1950s, and most of us want to enjoy that extra time, not have poor health due to a bad diet when we were younger.

What is worrying the government is that we are, on average, getting fatter. Even though we eat less food than in the 1950s and so take in fewer calories, we also use fewer calories. In the 1950s, many more people worked in factories. Now they sit behind desks all day.

In 1950, tea was the most common drink for children – today it's soft drinks, and they contain far more sugar than you would ever put in tea.

There is a big difference between what wealthier people do about keeping healthy compared to those with less money. There has been a great increase in the number of health fitness clubs, where people use exercise machines and swim to try to balance out the fact that they have not done much all day (picture ⑦). People with less money have, in general, not become as health conscious as those who are wealthier.

All parts of Britain now ban smoking in public places (picture ⑥). The number of people who have stopped smoking or who do not smoke has risen in older age groups, but it has not fallen among children. As cigarette smoking is a major cause of cancer, this is a worry for parents and governments.

▶ ⑥ Smoking bans.

▼ ⑦ A fitness club with exercise machines.

Glossary

BROADBAND A fast means of getting digital signals to move along ordinary telephone wires.

COLD WAR A time, beginning at the end of the 1940s and lasting until the 1980s, when the western countries such as the UK and the USA believed that the Soviet Union was a threat and that real war might soon come if they did not build up stocks of weapons. The Soviet Union believed the UK and USA were a similar threat.

CONSOLE A small computer designed for playing games. Its controls are joysticks and other ways of making things change quickly on a screen.

CONVENIENCE FOOD Food that has been prepared in a factory so that it only needs reheating, not preparing and cooking.

DESIGNER CLOTHES Clothes sold on the reputation of a particular designer. Clothes that sell on a name are also called branded goods.

IMMIGRATION The arrival of people from any country outside the United Kingdom (including the Republic of Ireland and other EU countries).

STRIKE A time when the workers in a company withdraw their labour.

TRADE UNION An organisation which is supposed to look after the working interests of its members.

Index